AS I WANDERED

As I Wandered

❧

Helen K. Hilliard

As I Wandered
Copyright © 2022 Helen K. Hilliard

All rights reserved. This publication may not be reproduced, stored in a retrieval system, or transmitted in any form, recording, mechanical, electronic, or photocopy, without written permission of the author. The only exception is brief quotations used in book reviews.

Comments prosencons@live.com

Cover Photo
Courtesy of Austin Bond

ISBN:
978-1-950768-79-0

Published by Prose Press
Pawleys Island, SC 29585
prosencons@live.com

Thank you to my family
for your love, inspiration, and encouragement.
Special thanks to my husband George and my daughter Heather
for their help compiling these literary works.

Contents

I. Family

A Little Old Lady	3
Angeles City Market	4
Awesome Surprise	6
Beloved Nephew	7
Bungee Cords	8
Buried Memories	9
I Remember Him	10
Bye Bye	13
Homecoming – A Sonnet	14
Company Came	15
Enjoy the Gift	16
Generation Gap	18
Here's to Jeremy	19
Happy Birthday Clara	20
Heather	24
Hugs Help	28
In the Ring Again	30
Joe	31
Last on a List	32
My Mother was a Giver	34
Neighborhood Talk	35
Swan Lake	36
Reservations	38
Thanks	39
The Sense of Mother	40
We Know	41
The Visit	42
Honey	45
Mother	46

II. Life

Acquainted with the Night (Robert Frost) – Response	50
A Glimpse of You	51

Alarm	52
American Landscape	53
At the Reunion	54
Awakened	55
Basket Case	56
Cardboard City	57
Carnival	58
China Plates	59
Connect the Dots	60
Don't	62
A Dreamy Message from Pen and Paper	64
Explosion	65
Fine	66
Gone Now	67
Good Catcher	68
Heavy Rain	69
Limbs of Life	70
My Secret Love	71
My Way	72
Never Mind	73
Not Quite Ready	74
On the Day the World Ends	75
Paseo Del Rio	76
Pride	77
Reply to – Harsh Words	78
Rescued	79
Reunion	80
Say a Little	81
Secret Service	82
The Christmas Trees	83
The Question	84
The Storm and Me	85
The Two	86
The Yarn	87
Priorities – A Villanelle	88

III. Love

A Husband's Gift	92
Angora Hat	93
Bonfire	94
I Felt Loved	95
Road Trip	96
Left	98

IV. Nature

Pay Attention	102
As We Wandered By	103
Great Blue	104
Beach Party	105
It Creeps	106
Snow	107
Speak	108
The Pathway	109
The Spirit of the Tree	110
Foam	111
Tree	112
Breakthrough	113

V. People

Babies on the Beach	116
By Invitation	117
Cupcakes	118
Next Time	119
ELVIS	120
Fred	122
Good-bye Johnnie	123
Indiscretions	124
Obituary Reader	125
Obstinate Herbivore	126
Mistake	127
Retired Chemistry Professor	128

Shipmates	129
Specials	130
The Sky is a Cloudless Blue	131
"U"	132
Upgrades	133

VI. Spiritual

Christians – Maya Angelou	*136*
Of Course – I prayed (Emily Dickinson) – Response	137
I Am	138
A Heavenly View	139
Heavenly Ballerina	140
A Spirit	141
Confined	142
Falling	143
Flee	144
For Us	145
From Supernatural	146
He Waits	147
New Day	148
Just Me	149
Fruit	150
In My Babylon	152
Dear Jesus	153
Presenting You	154
Questions	155
Pride Trap	156
So Busy	158
This is a Test	159
The Bible is True	160
Welcome Back	162
Idols	163
What is Christmas?	164
You Waited	166
Not the Bread and the Knife (Jacques Crickillion) – Response	168
Amen	170

I. Family

A Little Old Lady

A little old lady lives with me

Her face resembles, Nana,

My father's mother

She probably receives a

Social Security check

And may be on Medicare

I am startled by her reflection

Every time I pass a mirror

Angeles City Market

Dark hands reaching
for him from
among aisles.
What do they want?
Alleys narrow, filled
with almond eyed
merchants gawking, "hey Joe."
Stacks of fabric folded
forcing us toward bins of
bananas and melons.
Filipino umbrellas
opposed to the sun
piercing with prongs
as his tiny hand
just about slips out of mine.

"Hurry," I say,
stumbling past raw meat
hanging,
fish eyes luring us in,
owners stretching
arms toward him again.
Why did I come
alone with my son?
Then a hand landed
palm down on his head.
"Ah," it said,
feeling the wispy
threads of flaxen
so unlike
it's own.

Awesome Surprise

"Doesn't that guy out there look like Wes?!"
.........and Debbie
.........and Heather
.........and Monica

Happy Birthday To You
Happy Birthday To You
Happy Birthday Dear Mother
We Are Dancing For You.

With tears in my eyes,
AWESOME SURPRISE

How did you work it all out?
I knew nothing about it.

Two emeralds, a pearl and opal are mine.
Sharing all 6 of us how our lives are entwined
With love and laughter and listening too,
Look back 20, 30, 40 years through –
Memories of diapers and dreams and desires and dares,
Of problems and people and places and prayers.
The saying and sighing and singing and sharing,
Of camping and crabbing and crying and caring.

Touching hands, and hearts with so many hugs.
A little taste of heaven
That is how I see that it was
Two days full of love and fun!
Thank you my 3 daughters and one special son!

Beloved Nephew

The orange moon rose on
A horizon of hope while
The marsh water reflected
My faith in a harvest - not dawn
But at least a dream

Then

A tyrant of urgency entered
Interrupting my calm - interjecting
Wild wind and wailing rain
Pounding pain as I wondered why
The night you died

Bungee Cords

Elastic
Bouncing – forward
    reverse
Often with a hook
Occasionally used to tie us down
From time to time – dangerous
Requiring a harness
Disappearing out of sight
Ever to return
With a snap – springing back
Full of surprises these bungee cords

Our adult children

Buried Memories

She is ninety
Silent
Not sad
Sometimes silly
Content to sleep
To nod
With nothing serious
To think about

Her past
Sleeps like she
In piles of souvenirs
Sorting through
Seen as
Dusty pieces
Presenting themselves
Parties, passions, pleasures

Gone
To a grave
Never seen
They silently groan
To someone
Going through them
Then scream
To live again

But they won't

I Remember Him

my cousin
four or five
little blue sun suit
nothing more to do
than build sandcastles
by the seashore – with me

I remember him in
grammar school
geek with glasses
too smart – already
cracking jokes

I remember him with
our maiden aunts
back then – beguiling them
like an adult
he grew up faster than
the cousins he teased

I remember him
leaning out of
his parents' third floor window
the brownstone – seeing Billy Penn
we watched the Mummers Parade together

I remember when
he strutted too
James Dean he thought
black leather jacket
collar up
D. A. – tough guy
my mother worried
too much on his own

I remember him when
he was
finding his way – almost
afraid of him some days
he survived South Philly
after all

I remember then
one summer
he ran errands for my dad
At the print shop
his antics became
hot dinner table topics

I remember the
dapper college guy
independent I am
then the military man
then not – debating a lot
about life   his dad's death
puzzling over problems
with Mom – always the don
dealing with the aunts

I remember the –
searching for jobs
new relationships
the Italian attorney –
always ready to help others
host a fabulous feast
win an intellectual debate
I tried to relate
to this bachelor's life
deliberation – interrogation – consternation

but wait – fate
no – the Lord destined
him to meet
his sweetheart
we all know
her compassion and love
attracted him
blended well
with his quick wit and charm
her ready made family
fit him into
their lives – gave
him opportunity to experience
a family first hand
and land the role of grandfather
yes – who would have guessed

a unique individual
a special soul who
not only encouraged others but was
encouraged by the folks
in his church fellowship
nurtured by several

knowing a place of peace
with himself and God
smooth sailing for him now
wow – what a blessing
I am thankful
we don't have to say goodbye
Just – see you soon

Bye Bye

We celebrate your life
Good times as well as strife
We can picture you right now
Waving bye bye with a smile (at the end of the driveway
Even in the rain till we were far down the lane)
Even these last weeks – a little wave – the same
A final earthly wave remains
Till we meet again on a higher plane
We have a loss but you a gain

Bye Bye

Homecoming – A Sonnet

"Until the next of kin is notified."
I focused on the radio broadcast.
Was it I who qualified?
I longed for this agony to pass.

Did either of us really understand?
What sacrifice and woe we would endure.
Too close to acquiring the dreaded mourning band.
Quite of the consequences both unsure.

Through this we two discovered how to pray,
I, midst the care of children and the home,
He, dodging fire from migs and surface spray.
Tears stretched out to the unknown.

Escaping death and Hanoi Hilton he finally returned.
For obeying orders, by his countrymen he was spurned.

Company Came

stuck in a revolving door
another in pain
out of kilter all week
wrong level, wrong layer, wrong ledge
confusing classifications
no categories
stacked unevenly
never on top before
not my place
is there help available
scream at the same time
ignored, disregarded, overlooked
replaced over and over
vertigo setting in – sounds familiar
top disappeared
comrades kidnapped
missing friends
alone with aliens
help
who has been messing
in our kitchen
the same ones who have
been sleeping on the floor

Enjoy the Gift

"I have a surprise for you," my father would say as he arrived home still wearing his black brimmed hat and overcoat. I never knew what would be in the bag he held behind his back. My father was a generous gift giver who came up with unique choices. "Oh, daddy, thank you!" was my usual reaction.

When I was a little girl my father worked in center city Philadelphia. He often stopped in the stores along Market Street on his way to catch a train at the Reading Terminal. I believe he enjoyed purchasing gifts and giving them to me even more than I loved receiving them. Others often questioned his gift choices but I accepted and enjoyed using them. He bought me hats, jewelry, dresses, footlong pencils, decorated dolls, hot roasted chestnuts, large pretzels, and all sorts of items.

One day he presented me with a book about magic that came with a magic wand attached. My mother frowned at his choice but I was excited about the possibilities. I learned some magic tricks and arranged a performance for the family. There was a purpose for the gift and I enjoyed using it.

I believe this tradition of receiving gifts from my earthly father has helped prepare me to receive gifts from my heavenly father. Often the gifts are a surprise and rarely do they appear gift wrapped. Recently, I have been writing poetry. This creative inspiration comes from the creator God, my Father, and I take pleasure in using it. Sometimes there are people who question the origin or purpose of a gift, but they don't see the exciting possibilities.

Our Abba Father is similar to a loving, kind earthly father. If you did not have one of those as a child, think of mine when you receive a gift from your heavenly father. He enjoys giving gifts even more than you love receiving them. Wait expectantly for the next surprise He has for you – then thank Him and enjoy using your gift.

Generation Gap

I peruse the pictures
Not quite
Nudes

Of her
Plastered on the wall
Open for all

I read the ramblings
To a lover
Meant for none other

There now
For father and mother
Cousins and brother

Friends and foreigners
Those from
The past

Palm over
My Mouth
Gasping aloud

I log out
Of my granddaughter's
Facebook account

Here's to Jeremy

Celebrate my birthday and be happy – I am free.
My spirit is alive you know, some day you'll follow me.

But till that time when you find me,
In this much more perfect place,

We'll have to connect in some unique ways.
Just think of it as a more spiritual phase – so

See me in the glistening sand.
The rays on the beach and there I am.

Hear me in the laughter of my sons and I'm near.
Sense me in the love that together you share.

I'll be in the positive, kind words you say,
Encouraging others along a rough way.

You'll feel me in the warmth of a candle you burn,
Or a light in the window when you return.

I'll be in your cheers when the Phils run for home.
And in the shouts of the children playing in fun.

I'll be in your giving to others with love
And helping the helpless with strength from above.

I'll listen to your jokes and the nicknames you give
In the stories you tell about me – I live.

So celebrate my birthday – remembering I am free
Please smile – lift a glass – "Here's to Jeremy!"

Happy Birthday Clara

Well Clara is Ninety this very year.
She has given us much – so all yell a cheer

She has left some of you a little, and some quite a lot
So listen up and see just what you got.

But first stand up if you would not be on earth
If it was not for Clara and her years ago birth.

Now if you can't stand up just about every time
It's because you got many traits from some other line.

Like your father or mother who do not have Clara's genes.
Or her husband George Jr. who was on all the sports teams.

For sports she just watched her sons Alan and George
But she walked thousands of miles – onward she did forge.

So stand up if you too have a passion inside
For keeping in shape and lots of good exercise.

Clara was quite disciplined in all that she did
Perseverance she had since she was a kid

So stand up if you do things and always follow through
Like George and Alan and others of you too.

Now Clara was always spunky even when she was young
If you have a sassy spirit and perhaps a quick tongue

Stand up and admit it - your life is not dull
Even if stirring up the pot is not your main goal

Now these can admit that they are feisty some days
How about if you are smart in most of your ways.

Clara often showed she was good with her mind
So stand up if math answers you can quickly find

She also has always had a very quick wit
She makes others laugh or they take a hit

So stand up if you say things that people think are funny
Or you think your wit could help you earn money.

Now here is a trait that does take some flair
It is knowing how to dress and what to do with your hair

Clara was great at both of these things
She loved wearing necklaces, bracelets and rings

So if you have her genes for the knack of design
Stand up and let us see who we can find.

Now Clara also loved to watch a ballet
She dreamed of being a prima ballerina someday.

Do any of you like to dance on your toes
Stand up if you like ballet or have worn pink pantyhose.

How about playing cards – she was the best you know
Stand up if your card playing is good to go

Now her German blond hair that she had most of her days
Was passed along to a lot of you in many different ways

So stand up if you have inherited blond - colored hair
Even if it has darkened and is not quite as fair

Do you have big eyes that are close to blue
Stand up and thank Clara – that is what you should do.

With saving money and finding bargains back in her day
Clara was good – now what do you say

Are any of you good with money this way
If you are thrifty stand up and pay

Saving money is one thing, saving everything another
Clara rarely threw anything away – I discover

So if you like to save things and not throw away
Stand up so we can see what will happen someday.

Now Clara is generous and has always been so
She treats her family to presents you know

So if you are generous and give money away
Stand up – we want to know who you are today.

Clara sure did have energy and displayed lots of pep
When she was younger she on and on kept

Her energy was endless – she was always on the go
Stand up if you are peppy – we want to know

Clara has a love for animals – especially dogs
And took her own Rebel on many long jogs

If you have inherited this love for a pet
Stand up now for this is a good trait I bet.

How about a love for gardening and of the outdoors
Do you like to mow, weed and do other chores

If you stand up now, before it's too late
Some of us will let you work – we won't hesitate.

Her love for her family – everyone saw
She sacrificed and cared for one and all

If you love your family stand up right now
And give to Clara a formal bow.

There are probably a lot of other things too
That Clara has given to me and to you

Stand up if you are an in-law like I have to say
We would not have our loved ones – without Clara's birthday.

So we say happy birthday and thank the Lord so
For your life, Clara S. Hilliard as onward we go.

Heather

Such a joy in our lives, we almost forgot,
As an infant so colicky – you cried a lot.

A day or two old when we brought you home,
A tiny "squid" in a world of your own.

We walked and rocked you so you would not cry,
As you got older perhaps that is why,

You never stopped moving in crib or on trike,
Guess you were in training for a life-long hike.

This activity level only rose with the years,
Running here, climbing there – we did have some fears.

You walked at 10 months – before anyone else,
And wanted to do things all by yourself.

A "giraffie" you carried everywhere you did go,
Oh by the way, you sucked your thumb – did you know?

A big-eyed little blond girl as rough as a guy,
You didn't like dresses and weren't very shy.

You begged for a two-wheeler at 4, and at 5,
In minutes you rode it – your dad close beside.

You played with army trucks and some little men,
Never liked pretty dish sets or dolls way back then.

You spent time shooting guns, wearing boots and a hat,
Rode imaginary horses and wore real western spats.

You disliked any kind of spend the night party,
Got Mom to make excuses – you were a smartie.

Remember the time you first went to camp?
The tears you cried made your pillow real damp.

You were teased by your sister, but rarely fought back,
A genuine sensitive nature and that's still a fact.

Into fishing and tree forts and sports of all kinds,
Threw a ball better than most boys – that changed some minds!

Cut off jeans and ponytail you skateboarded around,
Wherever there was a pick-up game – you could be found.

You were the girl on the male team before it was vogue,
Your agility and ability took you on the road,

To being an all-star with no season off –
Volleyball, softball, basketball and golf.

There were other teams too, like lacrosse and track,
They asked for your help when they felt a lack.

Everyone wanted Heather on their winning team,
This caused your proud parents often to beam.

On time for practice – coaches counted on you,
You're still faithful and disciplined in all that you do.

Got your license the day you were eligible to drive,
Jumped in the car – and on that you did thrive.

Much more comfortable – a boy to be your friend,
This became a lifestyle, not just a trend.

You did all your chores and liked mowing the lawn,
You were Mom's right hand when dad was gone.

Throwing newspapers on your early morning route,
Taught you early in life what work was about.

With jobs at Busch Gardens and in Washington DC,
You are always successful – we're as proud as can be.

You daily rely on the good Lord above,
He led you to Madison to meet your true love.

And to start your career as attorney at law,
Or your bigger career where they call you "ma".

A loyal wife through thick and thin,
A mother of four who a prize should win.

You are helpful to parents, siblings and friends,
Stand up for your values and shun modern trends.

You give wise counsel to all who do ask,
Are natural and honest never wearing a mask.

You make things happen – that is your way,
Perseverance – "just do it" is part of your day.

Super woman at 40, What can't you do?
You rank at the top with only a few.

A Christian woman – God and family come first,
Providing an income without being immersed.

May God be glorified in your life as you pray,
May He expand your territory and keep evil away,
May His hand be upon you every hour – every day,
May God bless your next 40 in a real special way!

Hugs Help

Scrambled eggs in the slats of the clean kitchen chairs.
But Matt begs for a hug on the way up the stairs.

Ten trash cans, 9 bags are lined up out front.
But great singing and fun was presented by Hunt.

Parts of the plants and the flowers are gone.
But many errands were run by a nice guy named Ron.

Ashes from the fireplace land on white lambs wool.
But Jordan playing baseball looks really cool.

All the coffee was used from the pots that Mark made.
But a great performance the grandchildren gave.

While Christine and Zach tried tricking their folks.
Britton, Hamilton, Josh and Jordan rode the waves on their floats.

Wes and Heather disagreed on an issue or two.
But a grandson named Sam said, "Honey I'll miss you!"

Confusion and clatter were two of the themes.
Kathy observed and took pictures of scenes.

Nine hundred sheets and towels are now in the wash.
But what a pleasure to hear the trumpet by Josh.

The odor of dead fish and crabs fills the air.
But on the 4th of July it was fun with a flare.

The Taiwanese chest took many a nick.
But kids were quiet when watching a flick.

Sick tummies threatened to infect us all.
But Heather and Monica were the nurses on call.

Dan did not like it when he didn't get his way.
But amazed everyone with all the words he could say.

The lazy boy chairs took abuse round and round.
But jokes and laughter everywhere did abound.

The little ones would cry, run away or yell.
But Molly and Abby liked watching them and did it real well.

There now is a hole in the wall of the front bedroom.
But Debbie was always ready to man mop or broom.

Peanut butter, jelly and sand on the floor.
But a sweet " Hi Poppa" greeted us at the door.

Five thousand, three hundred, twenty-five spent for food.
But at meals the whole clan was in a good mood.

Crumbs in the corners and stains on the rugs.
But from Katie, and Kaylee and Gracie came hugs.

They are all gone now.
With hugs, I survived somehow.

In the Ring Again

Sparing with a heavyweight – a hard hitter
His footwork is fast – On guard
A jab to my jaw; tasting blood
I reel from a right; then a left
Nostrils flaring his eyes glare down
Numb on the canvas I remain alone
Mind struggling to remember
The trainer's refrain – what experts explained
Sudden strike to my chest worst yet
Riding the ropes with a mangled mouth
Bones tingling, unable to think
or speak I hear from around the corner
Comes coaching from somewhere
Midst the fear – "Keep fighting,"
"Never give up"
Tears burn on raw skin
on rubbery legs I rise
"Think punching bag," a fan yells
I pelt, pepper then pin my opponent
Upper–cut lower–to his gut
I Remember that
I am a fighter in this ring
A hard hitter - a heavyweight
"You can't have me," I scream
"I will not be defeated."
My fans are cheering
They hold my hands high
Finally - the malignant marauder
The stalker is getting weaker
He will not destroy me
Soon he will be down on the mat
Pounded out of me
When the final bell sounds
Who will be the winner?

Joe

> Faithful
> Forgiving
> Loyal
> True

I am thankful to God for a brother like you.

> Honest
> Humble
> Fair
> Kind

Not many around like you to find.

> Listening
> Loving
> Patient
> Wise

You have helped others as you advise.

> Prayerful
> Productive
> Caring
> Good

Thoughtful of people - doing what you could.

> Gentle
> Generous
> Funny
> Fun

I am thankful for the man that you've become.

Mom and Dad were proud to call you their son.
Now go with God as the rest of the race you run.

Last on a List

Lately I feel last on his list,
Left out.
Last on a list of grown children,
Grandchildren, pastors, elders,
Neighbors, friends, coworkers
Everyone.
All requests remembered, dealt
With right away, no delay
Taking responsibility
My name seems low on the list,
Maybe even last in line,
Left over.
Certainly don't disappoint them
Service workers, church members, visitors
Many more.
The office, the work, expected
Of course. For Tracy and Sheri
He'll hurry.
Sorry for myself I guess.
Selfishness is not nice I know
So?
Many demands on his time.
It is good I don't mind
Being alone.

Important requests,
Of course he is needed
By all.
Let's walk in the mall for exercise,
My share of his time.
Sublime!
The bills, the mail, the condos
All wail for his attention
And get it.
Is he married to others?
It seems so to me, church certainly
Am I jealous?
Well yes!
Never lets anyone down
All over town
Or country.
Just sharing my feelings
I know he is reeling
With requests.
Guess I will
Acquiesce

My Mother was a Giver

My mother was a giver. A humble woman who had dinner on the table at 5:30 every evening. She listened. She rarely talked about herself or complained. She was dedicated to her husband and children. She never had any alcohol. She rubbed my father's feet while he stretched out on the sofa. She read poetry to me when I was a child. She loved Jesus and said it often. She wore aprons, and prepared pot roasts. She did not bake bread but she put out pear salads and apple salads often. She never drove a car. She had the table set every evening. Her sisters and sisters-in-law were her best friends. She wore house dresses but dressed up every afternoon before my father arrived home. She moved furniture and changed the curtains with the seasons. She used slip covers on the sofa and chair in the living room. She did not speak when she was upset or angry. She rode in buses and trains, trolley cars and taxis. She walked down Mill Road to get the red bus which traveled from Lansdale to Chestnut Hill then back after her errands were completed late in the day. She rode the trolley car down Germantown Avenue to transfer to the L Bus which took her to Roxbourgh. She scrubbed the linoleum floors with a golden bristled brush and Namath soap. She heard me. She knew when I was troubled. Money in envelopes was her financial system. She ignored the negative.

I took after my father.

Neighborhood Talk

His Daddy died…

It is so…

Sad…

He is so…

Sad…

His Mommy is so…

Sad…

***

He is three years old.

He shouts across the yard

"My daddy is in Heaven and we are fine"

Swan Lake

Swans
    Appearing
        On the lake
    Floating
    Hovering
    Swirling
    Twirling

Girls
    Dancing
        On the ice
    Reaching
    Pointing
    Touching
    Reeling

We
    Watching
        From a distance
    Listening
    Feeling
    Tearing
    Waiting

She
    Presenting
        In white net
    Moving
    Embracing
    Gifting
    Giving

Skill
    Inspiring
        On the stage
    Acting
    Creating
    Working
    Wishing

Toes
    Crowding
        In point shoes
    Cramping
    Bleeding
    Bruising
    Pleading

Rest Lovely Swan
See You Soon

Reservations

"A Native American Indian Chief stands behind you."
The soothsayer told my father, long before I was born.

My mother who attended the Presbyterian Church
every Sunday scoffed at this.

"Did you know there is a large American Indian
standing behind you?" The stranger asked.

Daddy replied, "Yes he is with me all the time."
My ten-year old eyes opened wide.

Repeated another - years later.
"I see a tall Indian standing behind you."

Once, I took a picture of my father
standing with a Pawnee Priest.

They both sported clandestine grins.
In Oklahoma on the Res.

Does it make you wonder?
I have my reservations

Thanks

The balloons gave me a clue
But your laughter flew higher
Still lingers in the air
Flowers fare well
Faces reminding me of yours
Different personalities, philosophies
Blending perfectly into a bouquet
Thoughtful gifts – all good
Better, however, the gift of yourselves – being yourselves
How blessed we are by our offspring
The weekend celebration testified to that
Reinforced our gratitude to God
Thanks for sharing
Debbie, Heather, Monica and Wes
I love you!
Mother

The Sense of Mother

I see you again as I look in
My mirror

I hear you as I give advice to
My grandchild

I smell you when I use
Ivory Soap

I feel you when I cry
By myself

I taste you as I savor a
Serving of pasta

I touch you when my hands reach
To heaven

I become you as I perform
Household chores

I sense you as I talk
To Jesus

I think of you
Often

I miss you
Mother

We Know

Our happiest moment
The day you were born
You are standing here
Only our names show
With dates
Your heart beats
Tears speak
Love abounds
Needs no sound
Two butterflies nearby
We know

The Visit

They came for a visit, our four very own.
Debbie, Heather, Monica and Wesley our son.

We are so blessed to have them; they get along fine.
We love them a lot; we had a great time.

Our kids turned out real good; we appreciate them.
They care for each other remembering back when.

When they were together, the siblings four.
They've forgiven our mistakes and come back for more.

More memories, more fellowship, more food and more fun,
Making jokes about their father – Wes has many a pun.

We have pains in our sides from roaring so much.
Then remarks from the others like "you rock" and such.

Keep us laughing no matter where that we are.
In a parking lot with Heather driving the car.

Around and around in circles we went.
Her friend moving orange cones – the nice attendant.

The family dynamics are still there I guess.
"For ten dollars I dare you," kept coming from Wes.

"Vibrations" all good only Big Russ was bad.
Monz succumbed to the dares – Did it make people mad?

She climbed up to a window and glared at some folks.
Who were quietly eating dinner, just watching the boats.

Then we left her there and bent over to laugh.
She jumped down and said "I'm afraid of the staff."

I'm afraid people watching thought we were drunk.
If anyone knew us, our reputation has sunk.

"Let's make some coffee," was sort of a theme.
Debbie, Heather, and Monica, were the caffeine team.

They also acted as clothes consultants and therapists - who
said, "that goes, that goes, and so does that too."

The trunk under the bed is now history,
On top of the bed with mom lay sisters three.

Discussing deep subjects of life and of love.
Deciding we all need more wisdom from above.

The bed jacket remains on the bed post today.
"In case mother is bedridden" they said laughing away.

Parents, passive aggressive, picture taken, oh no!
"Cotton Picker" let's get ready for dinner and go.

Who's trapped in the "tomb" in the back of the car?
Mom always in front – the best choice by far!

Dad in the back yelling "what did you say?"
"For Pete's sake turn around and speak louder some way."

Wes was the techie with his iPod device.
Giving parents and sisters much needed advice.

He gave us examples of just where we stand.
Monica is in a chariot, horse reigns in her hand.

Deb needs only a radio in Sable (her friend).
"I'm satisfied with that – no money to spend"

But maybe there is hope; we're in the know now.
And we have new CDs burned by Wesley somehow.

We have learned some new words like "nano" and such.
And sing that new song about Big Bad Russ.

So thanks for the party and gifts of all kinds,
The ice cream, the candles and all of the signs.

The card – "it's only a matter of time- a few years
Till we turn into our parents." Does that bring fears?

Already the neighbor Whitaker mistakes Wes for George.
"You walk just like your father." Another gift from the Lord.

The big gift however for me and for dad.
A visit from our children – a blessing we had.

Honey

When I was in the sixth grade in Flourtown Elementary School
A girl named Honey rode our bus
The driver left her off at the corner of
Sunnybrook Road and Bethlehem Pike
Her hair was the color of the golden syrup and
Her name tasted sweet when I spoke it aloud
Only in my dreams would I ever have that name
She was so lucky
My name was Helen

Years later some of my grandchildren
Called me Momma
But one started saying Helen and it
Sounded like Honey so now they call me Honey
Or Momma Honey
Finally the thick golden liquid has
A home in my life
I am now called Honey

Mother
-Deborah Hilliard Piontek

Our angel in disguise
guiding, loving, praying
through every circumstance
that would arise

Always there for us
in the daily grind of life

Sacrificing, serving, settling differences
sewing dresses for us to wear
putting a pony tail in our hair

Through thick and thin
teaching, giving, helping
in every loss and win

Traveling near and far
sharing many sights
praying through lonely nights
when daddy was away
memorizing Bible verses with us to say

Birthday parties galore
camping trips to the shore
special memories for her four

Being together is important to you
even more so as your family grew

Waiting patiently
watching all of our activity
wondering what we'd turn out to be

Encouraging us to be true to ourselves
to do the next right thing
thank you God for what you bring
in our lifelong gift of mother

II. Life

Acquainted with the Night
— *Robert Frost*

I have been one acquainted with the night.
I have walked out in rain – and back in rain.
I have out -walked the furthest city light.
I have looked down the saddest city lane.

Response to – *Acquainted with the Night*

I have listened for the voice of no one near
I have touched ice until my hand is numb
I have felt wind whip through the frontier
I have observed tragedy in a Haiti slum

I have heard water over rocky shore drag
I have looked over a battlefield of fog
I have over-looked the raising of the flag

I have gone down in a lonely marshy bog
I have looked over a marshy muddy bog
I have felt wind whip through the frontier

I have touched ice until my hand is numb
I have heard waves crashing on the shore
I have observed life in a Haiti slum
I have prayed that I would see no more

Oh God help me see the light
I have been one acquainted with the night

I have looked over a battlefield of fog
I have over – looked the silence there
I have looked over a battlefield of fog
I have over – looked the raising of the flag

A Glimpse of You

A couple cuddles
A man's palm is
Placed on the lower
Body of the woman
Beside him
Another checks his
Cell phone messages
A baby's eyes stare at me
A woman's breasts
Are on display
A teen tosses her hair as
She walks up the aisle
My sight is impaired
Lord, it must require
Closed eyes
To get a glimpse of you
From here
In my pew

Alarm

Alarm rings
I'm dreaming.
No! It shouts. This is real.
A siren, a buzzer, a bell,
Hell, I don't want to wake up.
Blue light special at K- mart,
Get it. Get out of here.
Blue lights flashing
Surrounding me. That sound
Am I still dreaming?
Zur...ring
Wake up, wake up.
I'm dreaming don't wake me.
They are gawking,
A man reaches over and pushes me.
Wake up, Wake up.
I am dreaming, everyone watching.
I hear them shouting.
Wake up, wake up.
I stay there in my dream.
The alarm keeps ringing.
I ignore it.

American Landscape

Oil brushed silhouettes in
Dark hue navy blue and black
Standing indivisible
Barely recognizable
Paint long dried shows red some white
Colors bleeding into others
Commemorating shadows
Heads bowed against nimbus night
Hands raised to God offering
Their prayers for country and grace
Were efforts wasted by them
Where are they now and who are
These shrouded grievers of faith
Perhaps they are, Washington
Jefferson, and Adams, and
Hamilton, Madison, and
Franklin, forced on the canvas
Waiting for us to awake

At the Reunion

Misplaced on the Pennsylvania Turnpike
Between Fort Washington and Norristown,
Zen Buddhist Priest and Chemistry Professor
With combined degrees and accomplished reads,
Can't find their way back to a hotel
In Plymouth Meeting

Permeated with Nitrous Oxide,
Driving in circles, directions askew
They discover the art of going adrift,
Not this way - that - lost, yes.
What is the cost from exit to entrance?
Back again to the place where they started

Springfield High School replayed
From 1957 - thrown into an alternative
Universe, forced to find a way
Discover – they did
Confidently uncovered
The center of their universe

Now on level terrain at a crucial reunion
The loop finally closed
The toll has been paid
Epiphany extended to others as well
What the hell
It only took 50 years

Awakened

Awakened in the night she basks in the pure perfect light
    Unlike life

Brilliance from the moon streams through the years bringing memories of joy
    Some tears

Beams reflect the days illuminate the ways that life has transformed
    Her spirit

Moonlight streaks across waves white washing thoughts of being 63
    Not elderly

Reflected light intrudes on her sleep reminding her of laughter
    To give

Doom disturbs her dreams of the sunrise soon to come, more good to
    Be done

A shadow of gloom enters the room stealing her
    Breath away

A sweet soul is released to God just
    Before dawn

        She's gone

Basket Case

I jump, hoping never to hit the sides of sin,
never to be bruised, keeping arms close,
never touching, eyes closed to the
dangers within this cornucopia
upside down on end.
praying wire prongs
will never gouge.
welts do abound,
I've found, in
the narrow
end, of
this
barbed
wire
basket
I'm
in

Cardboard City

Cardboard City call it
My creation, my own, my home
Self imposed I suppose
Where size ten shoe once new
Now I am the stow
Away in a dark gray hideaway
From light and love
I fade away
This is not free
Oh so narrow a space
Can't see my face
Or hear my brain wave
To the outside from
My shoebox grave
Am I alive?

Carnival

No green gowns, just white and smiling
Carnival clowns abound in cubicles
Tossing balls, throwing darts
A party – I did see some balloons

No eyes closed or rose colored glasses
Just clear minds – keeping track of time
No anxiety here –
A circus atmosphere

More than 3 rings – mine is 16
No sedation except with beer
Funk and festivity everywhere
A good time – mine

No pajama-like smocks
Or tags with names
No clip boards or papers
To fill out – no questions here

Ferris wheel – no chairs appear
No canes or pain
Young people cheering
May I stay all day

Hey what am I saying
I wake up and see
They have completed my
Colonoscopy

China Plates

Picture a beautiful birthday cake with wonderful thick icing. I will cut a piece for you with a scoop of delicious ice cream on top. Now as you are thinking about that cake and ice cream and picturing it perfectly, let me see what I have that I could serve it to you on.

I delve deep into the wide wicker trash basket that I have in my kitchen and put my hand way down into the garbage from last night's dinner. Oh, there is an old paper plate. It is covered with tomato sauce stains and there are some smashed noodles on it, it is bent and torn, but still usable. I place the newly sliced cake on that plate and then top it off with a fresh scoop of vanilla ice cream. Want a fork?

What? You really don't like that idea?

OK. I go into my china cabinet in the dining room. I open the doors and pick a special white antique china plate. It has a gold rim around the edge and the center is shiny and clean.

I cut another piece of cake and put it on that dish. Then I top it with a fresh scoop of ice cream. A fork, and you are ready to dive in.

Yes. You say. That is much better. I will eagerly eat it now. Where are you going with this Momma? Oh, yes, I am going somewhere.

I am going to say that the birthday cake is life and it is served up to you as an individual. It will be your spouse someday and your children and your home and your job.

You are the plate.

Which kind of plate do you want to be?
If you are a clean china dish, you will enjoy the wonderful dessert of life much more than if you are a stained, dirty, old, crumpled, used paper plate.

A word to my valuable, special grandchildren plates from your antique grandmother.

Connect the Dots

Remember that childhood
Connect the dots sheet?
Do this in life
And your dreams you will meet.

Your goals you will see
By doing the next right thing
Though a small move
A trajectory it can bring

Don't worry about the big
Questions life throws.
Just take one small step
As the dot picture shows.

Why cry about the past
Mistakes you have made.
Just pick up the crayons
Make one mark on the page.

When each little dot
Is connected to another,
Dreams will come true
As you hardly bother

It is not the big drawing
That makes the big difference.
It is connecting little dots
Bringing the inference.

Just watch the dots grow
Turning into a picture.
A palate to color
In your life a fixture.

Don't

Substances I ingest
Alter my mind
My character
I like the sensation
I don't

Actions I take
Choices I make
Is that me?
Do I know who I am?
I don't

People I love
Others I hate
All mixed together
Do I know the difference?
I don't

My future, my past
Who is in control?
I want to be
Only
I don't

Anger, fear, pain
I feel them all
What do they mean?
Does anyone know?
I don't

A man, a boy, a baby
Do I need a rattle?
No, I am a man
Then act like one
I don't

I am something special
I am nothing of worth
Which one is truth?
Of course pick the first
I do

A Dreamy Message from Pen and Paper

The yellow lined legal pad calls to me softly.
The phone rings – loudly – off go the lofty
dreams of writing today.

I hear it again, then the cry of the pen
but messages for me and the answers they need end
any dreams of writing tonight.

To write – I intend to desire and do it – I must
Till into funerals and weddings and visits with people I'm thrust
Dreams of writing – they rust.

The paper and pen increasing their tempo and pitch
see me preparing and teaching, arranging and reaching – they switch
to dreams that will listen.

I hear all the clamors requesting my time and my mind.
The appointments, the meetings, the gatherings, the pleadings – they bind.
I ignore the dreams that are mine.

The empty paper continues to call – it's calling my name.
I hear it in the kitchen – I'm too busy is often my claim.
This is life – writing may just be a game.

Now a service man comes for something – just stayed and talked.
A nice guy but now I must start again – a new thought.
Competition for this empty page.

That cries out with pen – be in prison
a slave to us – use your wisdom.
Let life that is real do what it must.

Come dream and write with us!

Explosion

The atomic bomb
Over Hiroshima, Nagasaki
No solution, only destruction
Call the police, call 911,
Call Roosevelt, Truman, Eisenhower
A hole in a wall, a broken chair, the broken hearts
A nation being destroyed
A family floundering

The cloud hangs, floats
Life stops, stares
Stares at a fair-haired son
One born, raised to love, to care
Losing control in anger, despair

Falling debris, radiation, poison spews
Life flees, leaves
Life within dies and cries
For an answer, a solution
There is none
Where is the son

Ruins, piles of planks
Mountains of stone
Stench left behind
A mind destroyed
Can it ever be restored,
Rebuilt, renewed
Maybe
Someday
Pray.

Fine

Our friend finds out

He has cancer

Surgery soon

Internal organs out

He is thinking

We are thinking

Too much thinking

Gone Now

Drowning in a pond of tears
Thinking of our little pet
Gone now
A husband, a wife, 2 kids, a dog yet
Our Buddy
Did I even know then?
My dream the perfect scene
The importance of our friend
A beginning, not an end

Drowning in a place of tears
Thinking of our little pet
Gone now
What does he take with him
Our grey companion
I barely visualize
Do I even understand
Dreams demand
A beginning – must they end?

Drowning in a pool of tears
Thinking of our little pet
Gone now
Delusions show
My guilt spawned
Saturating my soul
Overwhelming me so
I'm sad -because I know
All beginnings have an end

Good Catcher

Put the leg guards on
Make sure your chest is protected
Have the helmet happening and
Your mask adjusted
Keep the mitt low
Now hunker down
With hands hopeful
Be ready to catch
The words that I say
Because in the next moment
I will not remember
The umpire will yell foul ball
The game will be over

Heavy Rain

A dark and driving rain -
An umbrella is needed.
I need an umbrella!
Hold it over me.
I am getting too wet.
It is pouring and I am drenched.
Even wearing a raincoat and boots,
I am soaked through and through.
A bigger umbrella,
Just won't do.
It is teeming now.
Bearing down on me heavily,
The wind takes it away,
My breath as I pray -
More trouble today.

Limbs of Life

Limbs of Life
Gnarled
Yet graceful
Misshapen
Yet majestic
Rough and worn
Yet poised

Limbs of Life
Knotty
Yet refined
Clumsy
Yet limber
Distorted
Yet Lovely

Limbs of Life
Complicated
Yet simple
Ugly
Yet beautiful
Pruned
Yet free

Limbs of Life
Reaching High
Yet slanted low
Dying
Yet Blooming
Patterns against the sky
Awaiting their fate
As I

My Secret Love

I desire you
I have made you require me
I need you
Oh I know you do
I crave you
Of course- I feed you
I can't get through life without you
I will continue to control you
I yearn for more and more of you
I am your secret love
You make me feel free
Oh but I hold you
With you I am bold though
Not so
I force you to go
In the wrong direction
You are really my possession
Bought by the devil of obsession

My Way

If they would only....

She should....

He could do better....

If they would just....

See it my way....

Do what I say....

They don't....

He won't....

So what

Give up

Never Mind

Never Mind
sugar is not borrowed
from neighbors or
notes not written
in real ink

Never Mind
people in faded photos
remain unknown

Never Mind
November crashes
into December
and the present
darkness wades through
marsh water till
it meets some
dawn beyond

Never Mind

Not Quite Ready

Not quite ready to
crawl under my blanket,
although
wind whips from
the Northeast,
catching me off balance,
like the Cat on a Hot Tin Roof.
Babies gone, along with
carpools and carnivals.
How long will it snow,
creating a mist
over the marsh.
Faster, faster
I can't see the beach,
two-piece,
blazing sun,
Newman and Taylor – gone.
That was June.
Spartina fades in October.
A vapor forms
till spring - then green.
What will then become,
Of me

On the Day the World Ends

On the day the world ends
I will be sure to make the bed,
All pillows in their correct positions
And I will Windex the kitchen counters.
I will walk hand in hand with
My man and discuss the flower pots
And the Santee Cooper electric poles
Being erected nearby.
I will have quiet time and pray.
I will walk 2 miles and mark the chart.
Yes, on the day the world ends
I will watch the NCAA basketball
Tournament games and an old
John Grisham movie called Rainmaker.
I will listen to news of earthquakes,
A tsunami wave train, radiation poisoning,
Charlie Sheen and Lindsay Lohan.
On the day the world ends

Paseo Del Rio

My dreams desiring
Like a river raging
Sinuous under the city
Hidden somewhat – yet aspiring

Has this river been there forever?
Ambition not showing
Beneath the streets
Under a bridge and then another

Running wildly unexposed
Wanting to be free
On its own
Some locks and dams imposed

Publish it for all to see
Stream of subconscious
Reality fluid
In a Celebration of festivity

Now a brilliant pathway by the river
As it loops and turns
Hang the twinkling lights
Tread the course together

Let the people come
Bring the mariachis
Set out tables for dining
A place for everyone

Enjoy the free flowing beauty
On the lovely Paseo Del Rio
Created by God
Not by duty

Pride

Are you going through a trial like Nebuchadnezzar of old?
Everything was perfect and now it is cold.

Read Daniel Chapter 4 and see what God did.
With Neb's prideful spirit it was not hid.

His "self" is the tree cut down in full sight.
Neb tumbled low very low from its height.

Are you going crazy and wondering why?
Remember the poor and do what is right.

Neb thought he was great and doing a lot.
But God wanted more and said you are not.

Not as good as you say so humble yourself.
Eat grass like the cattle; evaluate your wealth.

Look to me God said and Praise the Most High.
Not yourself and your goodness – stop saying "I."

Then Neb raised his eyes yes to heaven above.
And acknowledged God as the one he should love.

God's in control we've not done a thing.
He will humble and teach us His Glory to bring.

So please learn that lesson and do learn it well.
So you don't spend, like Neb, 7 years of pure hell.

Because God can do whatever he wants,
To show us his way in years or in months.

He may allow us to suffer till we get His point.
So beg on your knees for the Spirit to anoint.

And show just what He wants you to confide.
You may be surprised – it's usually **pride**.

Reply to – Harsh Words

Oh my dear poet there is hope for your tears.
For harsh words uttered and all other fears,

For hearts that are broken and nights without sleep,
For all of the words and hurts that cut deep.

For hateful actions regretted over time,
For the words that we have etched on our mind.

We all have negative events that take place,
Hidden thoughts behind a masquerading face.

For words we have sent like a swift flying bird,
For ominous silence – yes we have all heard.

If you have in your mouth a bitter taste,
From words you may have spoken in haste,

Spiteful words that can't be erased,
And you sense a metamorphosis taking place,

Then cover yourself and the soul that's been raped,
With the love of Jesus like an enveloping cape.

Hide under Him – find forgiveness and love.
Be filled with the Spirit of God from above.

Offer yourself and all your concern,
To the Great Triune God – that's how we will learn.

Rescued

Lying on cement
Folded neatly
Tucked inside itself
Enclosed in cellophane
Enduring rain
Heat, cold, snow
Alone
On the driveway
Waiting to be read
Understood
Rescued

Reunion

Mardi Gras
Halloween, whatever
Holiday it seems our destiny
To unveil our true identity
A time of jubilee

Wisdom now where puzzlement
Once barricaded reality
Remembering dream or nightmare
Like paper dolls we are
Cardboard sections jig sawed

Craving to connect back
Into that antique masterpiece
Bent, bulging, broken parts
Not quite the same fit
Distorting the total picture

Sharp edges removed
More rounded now
Sensible psyches
Grounded senior citizens
Enjoying this rite of passage called

Our 50th High School Reunion

Say a Little

Say a little
Smile a lot
Sometimes
That's all you've got

When others
Want to
Aggravate
Or agitate for naught

Secret Service

If service for the Lord is given
Money, time or deed
Better it be hidden from
The eyes of all to see
Better that it be discrete
With no fanfare or applause
Better that the motive stay
True and never false

The Christmas Trees

The
Christmas Trees
Fine firs, pines, cedars, balsams
Dark green with blue under the tent
The Lions Club member warms his hands over
The hastily made fire shooting sparks onto Highway 17
Majestic, fresh spruced up to sell ready to decorate the graceful limbs
We go at night with dad to pick out our perfect tree the tall graceful one
Tied on top of the car to take home and show mom our fine choice for
the tree this year

The
Christmas Trees
Fine firs, pines, cedars
Balsams, spruces dark greenish
Blue in the night under the tent or silvery shining
Strong trunks full or slender feathery with a light scent
The Rotary Club members warm hands over
A hastily made fire shooting sparks onto Highway 17
Majestic trees spruced up and ready to sell to the right family
Graceful limbs longing to be our perfect tree decorated tonight
Tied then on top of our car to take home and show mom our fine choice
We get home and find crooked branches and bruised limbs to hide in the corner
Against the wall gnarly branched disfigured limbs shorter than we thought earlier
Fill the empty spaces the holes with red balls cover up the bare spots where there are
Knotty wood and dead or sawed off bark where once seemed perfection what happened
In the light coming in through the window in our living room could this be
the same tree

The Question

What did you do with what you were given
You will be asked some day

That is the question that makes you accountable
For all that comes your way

It may be money, it may be time
Or gifts you can relay

But when the question is asked of you
What in the world will you say

The Storm and Me

Hurricane Ophelia is churning in place
Where will she go?
What will she do?
Oh storm off the coast – I feel like you.

Rain bands and thunder then some sun peeks through.
Winds of importance.
Direction askew.
Oh storm near the land – I feel like you.

We both cause disruption, turmoil and fear.
Hurt people around us.
We don't have a clue.
Oh storm stuck in place – I feel like you.

Let's hit the bottom and give up what we are.
Do what we should.
Look for the good
Oh storm striking land – I feel we could.

Let's both not look back as we blow out to sea.
Destruction behind.
New peace of mind.
Oh Storm leaving now – I'm going to be fine.

The Two

Town
Windows barred
Unkempt sidewalks
Methadone situations
Racial issues
Politically incorrect

Woman
Mind excluded
Disheveled Hair
Sanitary Situations
Monetary issues
Socially inept

Pride and purpose
Missing
Same fate
Town and
Lady found
Forlorn

The Yarn

Tell me a story
Spin me a yarn
With a long ending
About a horse farm

Write a narration
About some blue yarn
Tied up in a ball
Found out in the barn

Read me a report
Wrapped up in wool
Unraveled in a stall
That will always be full

On the table just now
But a future I see
Cast on the stiches
Knit 2 purl three

A blanket was designed
To cover a horse
Loving hands created it
For his warmth of course

Priorities – A Villanelle

If you were sure in only weeks of your abrupt demise,
Would you be reading rapidly this little rhyming scheme,
Or would you think of other ways you could prioritize.

Maybe you'd ask the question what to do before one dies,
Or dwell on all the years of life to act upon a dream.
If you were sure in only weeks of your abrupt demise,

Perhaps a weighted list's preparing would be wise;
Some actions of importance plus what they really mean.
Then you would know of other ways you could prioritize;

Becoming more authentic thus removing that disguise,
Being who you really are and not just what you seem,
If you were sure that coming soon was your abrupt demise.

For reasons obvious enough mortality does equalize.
Forgiveness and compassion to you great joy can bring.
Now might you think of other ways you could prioritize.

Just what kind of legacy will your family recognize.
Will you have regrets or have you the time redeemed.
If you knew that coming soon was your abrupt demise,
Surely you would think of many ways you could prioritize.

III. *Love*

A Husband's Gift

Colorless
Odorless
Tasteless
Like the air I breathe
This gift he gives me
Surrounds me
Enables me
Sustains me
Intensely hot
Cool and refreshing
Invisible yet effective
Powerful enough to experience
All I need from him
More than I deserve
What he provides for himself
What Christ bestows on the Church
This gift he gives me
Embraced in one word

Angora Hat

Christmas season
I was 12.
Caroling
Caravan of cars
I took a backseat.
He crowded beside
Girls giggling
He picked me
Heart beating fast
Face flushed.
Arms touched.

"I see now why you were so interested in going caroling,"
His mom said when she picked him up.
"Who was the little girl wearing an angora hat?"

Forty years later when she was in her 80's
She started calling me – Angora Hat.
I liked the nickname.
I still had the hots for her son.

Bonfire

Flames guarded when they could have expired
Burned out or escaped somewhere
Into a field of wheat blowing in the wind

Flames fanned when they may have flickered
Disappearing in the dessert
Covered by shifting sand and time

Flames stirred when they could have been cast off
Abandoned like cold ashes
Or feathers on a desolate beach

Yet coming from afar the fire burns
The sultry smell of smoke
Surrounds us as a spirit

Raya, Ahava, and Dod
Three flames burning together
Mingling our love

Friendship, commitment, and passion
The fire remains on the horizon
Kindled from above

Raya, Ahava and Dod –
the three Hebrew words for love
used in the Song of Solomon

I Felt Loved

He always, daily calls me cutie or hey beautiful and I love it even when I know full well that my hair is a mess and I have no makeup on. He whistles at me when he is following me and I feel loved even if I know that I don't have a body to be whistled at. He comes up behind me and hugs me when I am cutting radishes at the sink. He clears his dishes and straightens the kitchen when we have a lot of company. He works with me around the house as a team. He takes me out to dinner often. He shows concern for my happiness and contentment. He is loyal and tactful. He knows I appreciate him looking away from a display of boobs or ladies' underwear. He has confidence in my opinion and asks for my opinion and ideas regarding his business or church or community business. He listens. He teaches me how to be more organized. He shares his wisdom and what the Lord is showing him. He has a strong relationship with the Lord and prays. He spends time with me and socially with us together with others. He likes the kind of movies I like. He will go in and out of stores with me when we are on vacation even though it is not his favorite pastime. He is generous with his money and gives me freedom to get what I think I need. He not only compliments me when we are alone, but he says positive things about me when others are around. You are a good horse. Almost every meal he thanks God for the food and for this wonderful woman you have given me.

Road Trip

We are on an extended road trip
Our vehicle functions well
Not perfectly – stops at the jiffy lube or
For a complete overhaul when necessary

Driving on the interstate mile after
Mile   after mile   after mile
Passing scenes – too fast
Can't we stop somewhere? - please!

Sometimes we do recharge the battery
Inhaling mountain air, gazing into the valley
Browsing in antique shops, basking on the beach
Checking out the latest Broadway shows

Periods of silence – intense discussions
Speeders race by – we wonder why
Sirens sound around the bend
We spend time praying then

Eighteen wheelers on our heels
Sounding their horns
Stuck behind a dump truck
Flying particles attack

Thorny weeds cover the roadside
Searing sun rays
Invade – no shade
Re-inflating a flat tires us

We ride on narrow rolling roads
Darkness overcomes
Only our own headlights
To guide us – sometimes the moon

Rain pelts
Hail the size of golf balls
Thunder frightens – lighting
Streaks across the sky

After the downpour hear the
Breeze whispering – windows open
The ice cubes clink – a cool drink
Or something sweet

Mile after mile along the interstate
Or on a two lane road
A highway near shore
Blowing sand gets in our eyes

From across the dunes
Old tunes on the radio
When we hear them we
Smile and cry - sigh

Keep driving – till we arrive
Do we know our destination?
Yes – unfortunately
Keep on steering

Stay on the road
We are committed for
An extended road trip
Through time – together

Left

That day I was left standing
On the porch I cried
The dirty dishes languished in the sink
I buried my head in a pillow
The children dared not bother me

That day you left for a year
Was a hot day and I cried
The laundry piled high
I sat in a chair staring into space
The phone screamed unanswered

That day you left wearing your uniform
Was a dismal day and I cried
The moving boxes remained unopened
I lay on the bed lifeless
The dog barked unnoticed

That day he left – August 16th, 1977
You crossed the International Date Line
You never lived that day
Neither did I – and
Elvis died

IV. Nature

Pay Attention

The feelings you are facing
As painful as they may be
Tell you it's time to pay attention
To all around but "me"

Notice the sunset from the bridge
Or the dandelion by the path
The safest place to be is near
The battle is torn in half

Connect with other entities
Be they great or small
The lizard racing in the grass
Roses climbing a wall

Appreciate the warm spring sun
As it infiltrates your bones
And illuminates the darkness
Reminding – "I'm not alone"

Walk through a garden where flowers abound
Connect with the beauty there
God's creation will heal your soul
His Spirit will fill the air

As We Wandered By

The marsh marveled
As we wandered by
Spartina supposed
We were friends
Salt water waved
Near our feet
Pluff mud
Could not comprehend
This odd couple
As we wandered by
The egret and I

Great Blue

Great blue
among
the brown grasses of
the winter wetland
fog hovers
covering the scene like
a shroud
no hint of sun
shallow salt water seeps
down into
black marsh mud finding a
blue
heron hiding
reminding me
of myself

Beach Party

Shells and pieces of shell
are scattered like confetti
across the shore.
Mini bubble balloons
rise from the foam.
Wind plays a tune
while grains
of sand dance.
Pelicans pounce
providing food
from the surface.
Wave after
wave lingers
a little longer.
Gulls line up
at attention
ready for
the parade,
but there is none
at this winter beach party
for one.

It Creeps

It creeps like an egret
Through the grasses
Like fog over water
It hovers
A day without sun
Night with no moon
A thief stealing joy
If dwelt on too long
I could not go on
Here it comes again
Creeping
This sadness

Snow

Snow – silent, soothing
Soft in the darkness
Hushed on the hill
I walk through a hint of heaven

In the daylight
Glittering, gleaming, glaring
Sun burning my face
As I sled down a slope

Snow covering the earth
Cleaning the countryside
Cares disappear
It is snowing today
No school

Speak

Let the silence speak to me now.
The pluff mud is cool.
Is it green, spirited,
Pulling me under its spell?

My mind is a shovel digging,
Digging, deeper and deeper.
Now I am sinking into the
Mire, heavy and dark.

From under the oyster beds,
What am I hearing?
Is it marsh grass rustling?
Far above me?

The silence seems to whisper,
In lighted yellow tones,
Touching me thoroughly.
It seems to know me.

Listen to the stirring.
Is it just random black noise?
No, the more I listen, the more I wonder
Is that you God?

The Pathway

weeds
entangle
strangle me
along the path
brown strings
sticks decorated with
Lance cracker wrappers
lids stabbed
with straws
bits of pink plastic
insects crawling
vines gangling
Bud Lite cans
crushed among them
then
a face in the crowd
black - eyed
a Susan
smiling

The Spirit of the Tree

This branch
Of the banyan tree
Tricks me
Into thinking
There is a woman
Alongside,
Slim and sinuous
Arms, hands
Reaching high
Into the foliage
Of her hair
As it flows upward,
One with the wood.
I hear her soul
Her body curves
As she bends
With the branch
Growing together,
Back arched,
Stretching toward the light,
She is the essence of aliveness.
Bone, blood, balance, beauty
One in spirit
"One pathway…"
One in sisterhood with the tree

Foam

foam

forms on notes
of crashing majesty

floats as strokes
on a waiting palette

finishes like tears
on my face

foam

Tree

Look up

To see the future

Flourishing

Look down

To the roots

Unrecognized

Look in

To the bark

Distorted

Look out

For time

Rushes by

Breakthrough

The dune line holds
Except in one spot
Where the tide
Has changed the scene
Challenged the sand
Burst through anew
Filling the marsh
Flooding the grasses
Fooling the fowl
What now?

V. People

Babies on the Beach

Two in the sand – the sun
Knowing none of what life had to offer

Easy then for them – barefoot on the beach
More difficult days to come

Reaching into the past – we must laugh
Laugh at what time has done!

By Invitation

By invitation we followed
Narrow rural roads through
Southern Carolina where
Fields of lavender wild
Flowers welcomed us as we
Ventured farther into the pine forests

Meadows greeted us with brown, green, golden
Grasses flanked by fields of umber earth
an occasional aged tractor
an orderly residence, a trashed trailer
a dilapidated dwelling front yard piled
with possessions – dark men wave

a fire house a family road we found
Furman then the Trail McKenzies forged
to reach their fields
Three houses seen-serene
 a flag flying this would be the place
A ranch house – her mom and dad's renovated
White with a green roof surrounded by picturesque
Plantings – uniquely quaint gardens a peaceful pool
Did we hear roosters
Friendly greetings – good fellowship, flavorful food
Followed by a golf outing on the Penny Branch
Carved for family fun where the old farm had flourished

The clubhouse held tales of times past
Family history here midst the live oaks and azaleas
wheat and rye – Patches of the past –
Dear to them who hold it
Fun for us to understand
Magnetic memories
A delightful day

Cupcakes

Sweet Icing
Colorful
Quiet Cake

Take no action
Give no opinion
Never argue

Enjoyable
Easy to swallow
Yes

I like cupcakes
Better
Than I like

Most People
Including
Myself

Next Time

next time you'll notice them
slumped against the building
stucco unpainted
damaged doorway

kicking small pieces
of smashed concrete
through the dirt
middle of the day

leaning on an oil drum
corroded fire
stoking smoke
going astray

watching the sign
on the window broken
silently blinking
open café

staring eyes
gazing at you
driving through town
without delay

next time you'll notice
next time you'll have to
but this time
you look away

ELVIS

He captured the energy of my teenage years.
He made me feel like dancing.
He helped me forget my many young fears.
He taught me the words of romancing.

He sang about love for God and others.
He exuded a warmth that was catching.
He talked about loyalty to country and mothers.
He communed with looks that were fetching.

He shared his spirit reaching out to me.
He touched my soul directly.
He offered his singing so I could see.
He understood my feelings intensely.

I saw him appear on the Sullivan show.
I collected his 45's almost monthly.
I swayed to his music with my beau.
I grew in love immensely.

I "Love Me Tendered" and "Blue Suede Shoed."
I married and traveled around.
I to Elvis music was wooed.
I loved and was loved by the sound.

I went to his concerts, once on the front row.
I yelled and jumped with the rest.
I was a grown woman then I know.
I still thought he was the best.

I was lonely and sad when my husband went,
I remember - overseas for a year.
I knew what Air Force loneliness meant.
I dreaded that day with some fear.

I experienced overwhelming sadness I'd say.
I heard also Elvis Presley had died.
I had a double dose of weeping that day.
I sang "Heartbreak Hotel" and cried.

I recently traveled to his home at Graceland.
I wept most of that day too.
He was there in his spirit as I reached out my hand.
I felt his warmth in that place through and through

He captured the memory of those earlier years.
He touched my soul directly.
He reminded me to have no fears.
His spirit and God's joined effectively.

Fred

When I think of him
I see a word
An opening for others
Offering an option

He looks it
A long word
Not wide or round
The height of possibility

For you an open door to unity
With God and within
Introducing him
I've named him "opportunity"

Good-bye Johnnie

Saying good-bye is hard to do
I will miss singing God's song with you

But I will pray that you will sing
With other believers – much joy to bring

Stay in God's word every day
And tell Him everything as you pray

He has a purpose for your life
Look for His way even in the strife

Saying goodbye is difficult for me
I will miss your lessons coming regularly

Be filled with His Spirit and overflow
With His love so much that others will know

You are a believer in Christ our Lord
Always sing with Him in one accord

Saying good-bye is hard to do
I will miss singing God's song with you

Indiscretions

She never discussed
His indiscretions

She hid them
Under the mattress
Covered with
Chenille

She concealed them
In a crumpled
Handkerchief
Embroidered with roses

She tucked them
Deep in the pockets
Of her polished
Cotton apron

She veiled them
Beneath the brim
Of a hat, green felt
Stuck with pearl pin

She buried them
In the box
With her
Hurt

She never discussed
His indiscretions

But I knew

Obituary Reader

She died Monday
I had forgotten her
I now recall
A pleasant, quiet lady
Older than I thought – ninety four
Only seventy when I knew her
She moved to be near family
Like so many do
I may move away someday
People will forget me too
And I will die
But not today

Obstinate Herbivore

One turquoise
Equus burchell
Unique stripe
"What the hell
I don't give a damn; I am what I am
I'll stroll up this hill
to the 19th hole
Augusta National show
go against the flow"
And so
Captured – hauled off
Authorities toss
Into a cage
Not much of a loss
A zebra
Black and white stripe
Under the orange
Losing society's game
How strange

Mistake

"You idiot," the voice
Whispers
Realizing he is the victim
Of a scam
Wired money
Apple laptop to
Arrive in
3 days
3 years later he is
Still waiting
"Duped, incompetent"
The voice again
"You are stupid. You
Will never get it right."
Mistrust – not part of
His reality as a child
His private logic
A battlefield
Believe the voice
Don't believe the voice
Re program
Just a mistake
Somewhere out there maybe
An Apple computer
Lost in route
The battle continues

Retired Chemistry Professor

There he is,
the retired chemistry professor
with no inhibitions
twirling and twirling
the former cheerleader
their lives mingling
like cherry syrup
and Coca-Cola in 1957

"He is going to wear me out,"
she said, gasping for breath
he continued dancing
confident of his excellent condition,
knowing himself well
having achieved life goals
the dance floor is level
he closed the loop
at his 50th high school reunion.

Shipmates

Shipmates
Traveling together
One begins floundering
Losing Direction
Into the water
Thinking of the other
Dark and deep
Down and alone
Death is revealed
It has been chosen
God rescues him
Now she is on her own

Specials

Ed died
While we were on our trip out West
A restaurant owner
Just an acquaintance
He ran specials
Spoke with us as old friends
It has been several months
Since we were at his steak house
He ran special coupons in the Sun News
His food was good
His prices were right
His manner was friendly, familiar
His greeting made us feel important
We will miss him
Ed ran special

The Sky is a Cloudless Blue

The sky is a cloudless blue
The sea a glass tablecloth presenting antique lace at my ankles
I rub SPF 30 sunscreen on my face and arms
And stroll along the shore
The lace getting lost between my toes
This autumn day I think I am alone
A liberal allowance from the angels

Far up the beach I see a figure
I think it is a woman - playing in the sand
I squint to get a better look
She appears to be digging a hole
I strain my eyes to get a better look
There are high mounds of sand around her
As I get closer I see that she is standing waist deep
In the hole – I keep walking in her direction
I stop for a better look – now she seems
slumped In the hole looking
Like a rag doll slammed down by the wind yet
The air appears calm
The soft sand seems to be shifting and slowly flowing into the hole
her legs are already covered
I begin running towards her realizing
The sand is closing in on her arms
Moving up to her chest caving in on her
"Get up, get out of the hole," I yell
I don't think she can hear me
I am still far down the beach
   "Help – someone get a shovel" I yell to no one
I am losing my breath seeing that the sand will soon cover her
I don't have a shovel, I am too far away
God, isn't there someone who could help her?

"U"

Easy to push
U
into
Text or Twitter
U
Work as a vowel
U
Pair up so well with others, are
U
Ever yourself?
U
Are all about relationships
U
Become whoever I am with
U
Are anyone at all
U
Can be whoever
U
Want to be, but no matter how hard you try
U
Can never be me

Upgrades

He upgraded every few years,
The Chrysler New Yorker for instance,
His pride shown in the shiny black finish,
Its chrome spread like liquid silver under his hands.

She never knew when
His ego would spout a newer version,
One with more trim, bigger head lights, higher
Horse power, a new style with white walled
Tires and stereo. She was not consulted though.
Being, herself, a non-driver.

She had dinner on the table at five every night
Complete with pear salad on lettuce leaf
And mayonnaise. She was the perfect wife.

Over the years, not just one but a few
Models appeared beyond the kitchen
Window as she looked the other way
Wiping her hands
On the apron she wore
To keep herself unscathed.

VI. Spiritual

Christians
- Maya Angelou

When I say... "I am a Christian"
I'm not shouting "I'm clean livin'."
I'm whispering "I was lost,
Now I'm found and forgiven."

When I say... "I am a Christian"
I don't speak of this with pride.
I'm confessing that I stumble
and need Christ to be my guide.

When I say... "I am a Christian"
I'm not trying to be strong.
I'm professing that I'm weak
And need His strength to carry on.

When I say... "I am a Christian"
I'm not bragging of success.
I'm admitting I have failed
And need God to clean my mess.

When I say... "I am a Christian"
I'm not claiming to be perfect,
My flaws are far too visible
But, God believes I am worth it.

When I say... "I am a Christian"
I still feel the sting of pain.
I have my share of heartaches
So I call upon His name.

When I say... "I am a Christian"
I'm not holier than thou,
I'm just a simple sinner
Who received God's good grace, somehow!

Of Course – I prayed
- Emily Dickinson

Of Course – I prayed –
And did God Care?
He cared as much as on the Air
A Bird – had stamped her foot –
And cried "Give Me" –
My Reason – Life –
I had not had – but for Yourself –
'Twere better Charity
To leave me in the Atom's Tomb –
Merry, and Nought, and gay, and numb –
Than this smart Misery.

Response to – *Of Course – I prayed*

Of Course – I prayed –
And did God Care?
He cared enough His son to Share
A Lamb – the Christ who died
I cried – *"Give Me" –*
My purpose – *Life –*
I would not have – *but for Yourself*
This Gift – Eternity
To rescue me from Adam's Tomb
Merry and Nought, and gay and numb –
From this misery exhumed!

I Am

I am walking the corridor
From the parking garage
I hear greetings from those passing by
I understand surprise when
A different nurse appears
I suffer the rigid press
The edges of the mask
The table rising

I am more powerful
Than any radiant beam
Love - deeper, higher, wider
I permeate the heart
Discover imperfection
Forgive rejection
I am always present

I heal the soul
I am alpha, omega
Beginning, end
Best friend
I am the great "**I Am**"

A Heavenly View

An early morning mist hovers over the marsh.
A heavy evil force hiding the view of inlet, water and reeds.
It hangs from the hazy sky in silence.
No life, no love, no light.
It holds back the pink hue on the horizon.
Wait!
There is hope.
Like fire the sky turns orange, golden, bright.
The sun has risen to have final victory.
A heavenly view is in sight.

Heavenly Ballerina

Lively and Lovely
She dances
In light.

Whirling and Wonderful
She appears
In white.

Sleek and Soaring
She stretches
In sight.

Radiant and Rare
She flows
Just right.

Fair and Favored
She inspires
In flight.

Magnificent and Mysterious
She moves
With might

A prayer for this ballerina as she twirls through her life:

God, please shine on her with your light and provide for her righteous robes of white as you cleanse and forgive her. Always place your hand upon her, Lord, that she may keep you in her sight. Oh, Lord please fill her with the wisdom and love of Jesus so that she knows what is right. And Father, give her the Holy Spirit's power so she may take flight in you all the days of her life. Finally, Lord, keep her safe from the evil one with all of your might.

A Spirit

A spirit
He speaks in spirit and in truth
He creates, forms, flows
In and through

A soul
I sense and know the shape
I take the lead and follow
I do

A spirit
He floats, flies high
Soars like an eagle
Strong and true

A soul
I repent, confess
I listen and pray
Renew

A spirit
He glides through space
He forgives with grace
Mercy too

A soul
I worshiped in his presence
Bowed my heart
And grew

A spirit
He embraced
He enfolded
He knew

A soul
I am grateful
I praise
Thank you

Confined

I find
A monastery
A library
A sanctuary
A conservatory
Cloistered
Sanctified
Inspired
Educated
Energized
By my creator
To pray
To Listen
To Read
To Worship
To Sing
To Appreciate
Many choices
Open my heart
Lord
To your energy
Your ideas
Your path for me
Thank you Lord
For this prison

Falling

Falling
Falling
Falling
Away
Small Pieces everyday
Don't you remember?
I told you that
What is her name?
Help me remember
What was explained?
The word I want
Drifts away
Falling
Falling
Falling
A simpler word
Is what I say
But it's not what I want
Numbers transpose
I must be blunt
Digits, dates
Wait
That's not right
I cry out
From a height
Falling
Falling
Falling
Where am I going?
Catch me Lord
You won't forget

Flee

Do you remember Joseph the bold
Who fled from Mrs. Potiphar in the Bible we are told

Do you know the Mrs. Potiphar
In your life today?

What is your Mrs. Potiphar
What should you flee today

Is it gossip, lust, or something else
What does God have to say

Well flee from your Mrs. Potiphar
Whatever that temptation be

The good Lord says – obey my child
Run straight to me

Remember oh remember the Joseph who was bold
Who did not fear but trusted God
And to temptation did not fold

Not even to Mrs. Potiphar
Not even to the sin

That was right there before him
He never no never gave in

So when you meet a Mrs. Potiphar
Whatever it may be

Don't forget what Joseph did
And flee, flee, please flee

Oh by chance do you remember the Joseph of old
Do like him and flee from sin into God's strong hold.

For Us

From a heavenly height
You are God, God, God
Set aside divine right
To step on our sod

Became a servant
A person as we
Dependent on the Spirit
But no sin in thee

Demonstrated to us
God's Power and love
At least to the extent
We are capable of

Your death in our place
Life forever a gift
The distance from holiness
You came to lift

Jehovah our savior
Now judge and Lord
Father, Son, Holy Spirit
In one accord

For the Glory of God
Exalted your name
Gave you highest place
You are Jesus who came
For us.

From Supernatural

Pluff mud – cool and natural
pulls me into surreal
silence. Mind-digging brings a tear.
Sinking into the purest
place, a dark stare
turns to a whisper, so unreal
it creates an altar
of yellow tones, to nurture.
Random black noise from a star.
Or could it be lunar.
A far off quality, strangely paternal,
speaks and I am unsure.
I listen closely; hear its luster.
Is the voice eternal?
Might God be near?

He Waits

He is waiting for you.
                Every day He waits.

Once in awhile you drop by
                for a casual visit.

It saddens Him that you
                forget about Him.

He realizes that He
                needs to prepare you

For eternity.
                So, He waits.

New Day

New day
Same sun
Moving you on

New day
Same Father
Filling with faith

New day
Same Spirit
Showing through you

New day
Same Son
Moving you on

New day
Same Triune God
Three in one

Just Me

Impress me
Says the Lord
Yes, yes
Impress
Just me

Fruit

In Luke 13 does He mean me?
The one that bears no fruit.
Am I that tree that gives no figs?
Am I so deaf and mute?

Does He appear again and again
To check my progress daily?
And disappointed goes away
When He sees that I am failing.

Does He suggest I be cut out?
That I'm just taking space,
Because I'm not producing fruit
That I am just a waste?

Perhaps, but then the gardener
(That would be Christ the Lord)
Suggests to not give up on me
Another chance affords.

Another chance to be forgiven
To see the truth anew,
To read the word and pray more
Not worrying about what to "do."

Give up the fruitless, anxious life
Let Christ have half a chance
To change me – over and over again
Forgiveness my life will enhance

Search for truth, accept His Grace
And open up my heart
Don't be a fruitless, green fig tree
Pretending to be smart

You chose me, Lord, to bear some fruit
If I'm to follow you
What is the fruit I should produce?
What is it I must do?

It is not what you do dear child
This fruit we speak about
It is what's in your heart you know
That affects what does turn out

God tells you what to look for
In Galatians five twenty two
Love, joy, peace, patience, kindness, goodness,
Gentleness, faithfulness and self-control.

In My Babylon

In my Babylon
I sometimes weep
For the place I know is home
The place the Lord
Will always keep
After on this earth I roam
A place of love and purity
Where no sin is ever found
A place where free
Is really free
And does not keep me bound
A place called New Jerusalem
I sing of it today
As I am captured
In this foreign land
Where I love and work and play

Dear Jesus

You meet with me; you always show.

You bring to mind what I need to know.

You pull me into your loving care.

You give me peace just being there.

You calm my thoughts and heal my pain.

You make me very glad I came.

You listen to my feeble words.

You reassure me that you've heard.

You long to hear my praise and prayer.

You send your power to me there.

You want my thanks to be sincere.

You send your Spirit oh so near.

You hear my requests before I ask.

You answer prayer; it is no task.

You are the great "I AM" I know.

You meet with me; you always show.

Thanks

Presenting You

The distraction of discomfort
The dulling of my senses
To the world around me
The pulse pounding pain
Surrounding

Praying for direction
A way through the maze
Not only for endurance
On the edge of endness
But a way through it
Extending

Include me Lord
In seeing the love
In each moment
The lofty lovely line
Of angels in my mind
Leading me away from the pain
Presenting
You

Questions

Who can we trust
Why do we live
Who can we believe
What are we missing
Where are we headed
What is our purpose
How do we find peace
When will our lives end
Are there any answers

Lord, thank you for
The questioning
The seeking
The finding

Pride Trap

What are you proud of
Watch
Beware
It may be something that grabs you
Unaware
Like
Possessions
Reputations
Achievements
So much
Your family
Your friends
Who you know and such
Or it could be
Actions
Reactions
The work that you do
Your goodness
Your morality
Generosity too
Impressions
Concessions

Kindnesses
Even love
Thoughtfulness
Service
Blessings from above
Sound Strange
But Beware
What the evil one does
To twist us and turn us right back to self love
Beware
When you use the cunning word- "I"
Give it to the ONE God – the father Most High
Say to him "I confess" so humble me now
And he will change you oh yes He does it somehow
But beware
The snare
That Satan will set
To catch
You
In his ever ready
Pride trap

So Busy

phone calls, job, arrangements
cleaning, travel, laundry
kids, carpools, cooking
papers, appointments, yard work
bills, e-mail, exercise
eating, entertaining, repairs
errands, people, problems . . .
deeper
deeper
deeper
this snow never melts
as I plow a path
continually
trying to reach you
Lord

This is a Test

This is a test

God knows

It may not seem so

But it is

This is a test

God knows

Will you pass?

The Bible is True

So we've unlocked the code and we've proven the facts
That the Bible is true and that history's not lax

We've known about Gnostics, false gospels and such
Secret societies, phony parchments – a hoax, that much

We surely understand with all of this proof
From history and media of what is the truth.

What I can't understand is why we aren't telling
About His spirit within us – always dwelling

How He makes us at times want to stand up and shout
How He tells us and shows us what life is about

How He gives us wisdom when we have none of our own
How He points the direction when we are alone

How He fills us with his strength when we are so weak
How He gives a patient spirit when we don't feel meek

How He answers our prayers and shows us the way
How His very existence gives us strength for the day

How He lifts us on high to a mountain-top height
And in a dark valley, how He gives us light

How He allows us to gaze upon His perfect face
And shows us His forgiveness, His mercy and grace

Why aren't we even mentioning all the answered prayers
How He speaks to us inwardly and listens to our cares

How His love takes us over and fills us to the brim
Showing us clearly that it's all about Him

How He gives us words to say when we don't have any
How He changes our desires down to the penny

How about the fact He's our best friend
And we know He is with us and will be till the end

How His spirit lives within us and witnesses to our own
No hoax, but a proof when we are alone

So to Dan Brown and others who say Jesus is false
We say you don't know Him because you are lost.

Welcome Back

Welcome back myself – first love
Having been encouraged to forget
Have you been to war my dove
Welcome back myself – first love
How grateful I am to God above
Not to be forgotten yet
Welcome back myself – first love
Our reunion I will not regret

Idols

What are we doing?
Worshiping, sacrificing
To Idols
Of our own making

Giving time and money
Honoring their desires
Higher and higher they climb
In our eyes

Bow before them
Deify, adore them
Making sure they are
Gratified all the time

Bona fide?

Beware our own offspring
Are becoming the Idols
Of which we are warned
In First John 5 verse 21

What is Christmas?

Singing
Shopping
Thankfulness
Family
Turkey
Pumpkin pie
Football

No, that's Thanksgiving

What is Christmas?
Celebration
Parties
Parades
Fireworks

No, that's Fourth of July

What is Christmas?
Love
Joy
Greeting cards
Decorations
Hearts

No, that's Valentine's Day

What is Christmas?
Caroling
Giving gifts
Helping others
Church pageants
Santa Claus
School programs
Good fellowship
Twinkle lights

Oh, Christmas is really so much more
It's for us the great God's open door

You Waited

I left you there
Where you always wait

I left you there
Like a friend by the gate

I left to do
The many things that be

I left to do
The good that called to me

You came to meet
But I just rushed on by

You came to meet
I greeted briefly with a sigh

You came to give
Some strength for the day

You came to give
I went my way

But praise your name
You waited there
Till I returned to you

With repentant heart
With weary soul
Our covenant to renew

Not the Bread and the Knife

You are the bread and the knife
The crystal goblet and the wine.
      - Jacques Crickillion

Response to – *Not the Bread and the Knife*

You are the bread and the knife
The crystal goblet and the wine
You are the ball of orange on the horizon
The stack of puffs forming across the waterway
You are the pulpit in a country church
And the wood stork heading north

However you are not a field of sunflowers
Or the 1939 Oldsmobile Club Coupe at the antique car show
You are not a balsam breeze in the North Carolina mountains
Or a jar of almonds on the kitchen counter
No way are you a jar of almonds on the kitchen counter

It is possible that you are a gator crawling up from the marsh grass
Or maybe even a great gray heron on the prowl for food
But not even close to being a teabag floating in a cup of hot water
And a quick glance in the mirror
Will show that you are not the glass lamp on the table
Or the garden gloves hanging in the shed

It may interest you to know that
As I am writing this
I am the breeze batting the palm fronds
Against the bedroom window
I also happen to be a leaf blowing down the bike path
A feather floating on the sea foam at Huntington Beach State Park

Sometimes I feel like the sunlight behind a cloud or
The newspaper waiting on the driveway
Wrapped in cellophane and tied with a rubber band

But don't worry I'm not the bread and the knife
You are still the bread and the knife
You will always be the bread and the knife

Not to mention the crystal goblet and somehow the wine.

Amen

Conscious or Unconscious
Vapor appearing where
Air – like a Thief in the night
Steals Gold - mine – dig
Now or later – inner or outer
Space never faced - never explained
Restrained– unseen
Ruler of life – Dictator – Queen
Bullet – speeding Silence of a
Cyclone Center
Fantasy of the mind - unwind
Somewhere between
Unconscious and Conscious
Alpha – Omega, Beginning – End
It is Time
Infinity - **Amen**

CPSIA information can be obtained
at www.ICGtesting.com
Printed in the USA
BVHW042046151222
654320BV00008B/377